Prayer

Text by Inos Biffi
Illustrated by Franco Vignazia

WILLIAM B. EERDMANS PUBLISHING COMPANY
GRAND RAPIDS, MICHIGAN

Originally published as
La Preghiera, copyright © 1993
Editoriale Jaca Book spa, Milan.

English translation copyright © 1994
by Wm. B. Eerdmans Publishing Co.
255 Jefferson Ave. S.E., Grand Rapids, Mich. 49503

Printed in Italy

Library of Congress Cataloging-in-Publication Data

Biffi, Inos.
[Preghiera.   English]
Prayer / text by Inos Biffi ; illustrations by Franco Vignazia.
p.   cm.
ISBN 0-8028-3759-X
I. Children—Religious Life.   2. Prayer—Catholic Church—Juvenile literature.
3. Catholic Church—Doctrines—Juvenile literature.
[I. Prayer.   2. Catholic Church—Doctrines.]
I. Vignazia, Franco, ill.   II. Title.
BX2371.B5413   1993
242'.82—dc20   93-41090
                                                                      CIP
                                                                      AC

Imprimatur
in Curia Arch. Mediolani die 3 Julii 1993
Angelus Mascheroni
provicarius generalis

INOS BIFFI is Professor of Medieval and Systematic Theology at the
Theological University of Northern Italy, Milan.

FRANCO VIGNAZIA lives in Italy and is an illustrator, painter, and
sculptor. He also teaches art in the secondary schools.

Unless otherwise indicated, all Scripture quotations are from the New American Bible,
© 1986 Confraternity of Christian Doctrine, Washington, D.C.

Contents

The Sign of the Cross, Glory Be to the Father, The
Hail Mary, Angel of God, Eternal Rest,
Morning Prayer,
Blessing of Food,
Evening Prayer,
Hail
Holy Queen

Introduction

If a person does not pray, the Apostles' Creed loses all meaning, it becomes impossible to observe the Commandments, and the Sacraments produce no positive effects. That is why we published this fourth part of the Catechism and dedicated it entirely to prayer, which is the living dialogue with God and the response to his grace.

We begin this book by explaining when and how prayer was born and why humanity is religious. Then we recall those individuals who, according to Holy Scripture, are the ideals who show us how we should pray. Above all, however, we explain the prayer of Jesus, the great offerer of prayer, who expressly taught us to pray in the Lord's Prayer. Next we go on to discuss the prayers of the Church and the various times and ways in which the disciples of the Lord address God. In the last part of the book we include the simplest and most common prayers of the Church. When one memorizes these, one has a precious treasure for one's entire spiritual life.

The illustrations that accompany the text help clarify the discussion. Still, it is intended that children read this book under the guidance of parents or catechists, who can explain and add to the material presented here. But adults can help children grasp the message of this book most effectively by praying with them. This will initiate them into the regular practice and pleasure of prayer. Then prayer will become like bread to them, something that restores and nurtures them daily.

Humanity in Search of God

All of us feel the call of God within us, even if it is in a vague and confused way. All of us read God's message in our own hearts and in the universe that surrounds us, and it is like listening to God's story.

It was God himself who created human beings from nothing, and who imprinted in us the tendency to seek God, the need to pray to him, and a constant uneasiness until we are with him. "For in him we live and move and have our being" (Acts 17:28).

It is our nature, then, to be religious, and God is not far from us. However, sin makes our journey toward God difficult, and along the way we often make serious mistakes. But God has made us so that we might seek him, "even perhaps grope for him" (Acts 17:27).

Our religious nature explains so many things about human culture: the origin of religions, the building of holy places, the setting aside of temples dedicated to prayer, the offering of sacrifices, the variety of rituals, the books about and formulas for prayer. However, our sinfulness explains why, instead of adoring the one true God, we have created so many idols and worshipped them instead of the Father.

The Covenant between God and Humanity

Before we could seek God, it was God who sought us. From the very beginning, when God created us from nothing, in his own image and likeness, he gave us the gift of his grace, of his friendship. God did this because of Jesus, his Son, who became a human being.

God revealed himself to human beings by speaking to us in the depths of our hearts and through his creation, which is the work of God's hands and the proclamation of his glory. Our proper response should have been adoration, praise, and thanksgiving. However, instead of praying in joy and appreciation for the gift that we received, we proudly withdrew into ourselves. This is the sin of humanity, yet God has not abandoned us. With the promise of the Savior Jesus, God in his mercy began a history of offering humanity a covenant and forgiveness of our sins. The history of our relationship with him is also the history of prayer.

The Acceptable Gifts of Abel and Noah

Prayer is born in us when we become aware that God has created us from nothing. The first feeling that pervades us is, therefore, adoration, in which we recognize God as the Eternal One, the Infinite One, the Almighty, the Holy One. Yet, though God is high and holy, he has always been close to us, his creatures: he calls us to life and gives us everything because of his love for us.

Prayer is thus a response of gratitude and thanks-giving. This gratitude wells up from the depths of our hearts, the source of prayer, and we express it here before we express it in words or actions. But we also feel the need to show our adoration and gratitude through deeds. Thus, Abel offered the first-born of his flock to God, who appreciated that sacrifice as an expression of Abel's innocent soul. In the same way, Noah and other righteous people like him would sincerely honor God. But God did not appreciate offerings from those with impure motives. God did not accept the offering made by Cain, for example, because he could see that Cain did not have a pure heart.

The Prayers of Abraham and Moses

Abraham, the friend of God, stands out as one of the people in the Bible most dedicated to prayer. Abraham's devout nature can be seen in how attentively he listened to the Word of God, in his trusting acceptance of God's promises, and in his steady faith. For Abraham, prayer, which was time spent in the presence of God, was life itself.

Moses was also a great man of prayer. God spoke to him as a friend, "face to face" (Num. 12:8), and in the solitude and silence of Mount Sinai, where he received the Ten Commandments, Moses spent a long time with the Lord, begging him to forgive the people who had chosen to adore the golden calf rather than the true God.

The Prayers of Elijah, Job, Jonah, Hannah, and David

Sacred history is a history of prayer by the faithful, who through their faith welcome the divine gifts of the Word and of grace. We recall the ardent prayer of love and devotion that Elijah, the solitary prophet, prayed to God on the mountain. In response, the Lord came close to Elijah and spoke to him.

Job was also a man of prayer. The Lord put Job's faith to a long and severe test by taking everything away from him. But, although he had some very painful experiences, Job maintained his faith in the mysterious and wise actions of God.

When the prophet Jonah was on a storm-tossed boat, he was thrown overboard and swallowed by a large fish. He prayed for the Lord's help, and God freed him from the fish's stomach. In the same way, the tearful and humble pleas of Hannah were answered when God granted her the gift of a son, Samuel.

Above all, however, it was the prayer of the Psalms that rose up to God throughout the centuries of salvation history. It is thought that most of the Psalms were written by King David, but their song is heard at every liturgy of the Church even today. Over time they came to form the greatest prayer book of all: the Psalter, or Book of Psalms. In the Psalter, God has given us prayers for every situation.

Signs, Places, and Times of Prayer

Since God is spirit, and prayer must originate in our hearts, we can encounter God anywhere and at any time. However, he also speaks and communicates himself to us through signs, which make us aware of his presence. For the Israelites, a special sign of divine presence was the Ark of the Covenant, which they carried with them during their many wanderings.

The Israelites, who were a people of prayer, offered their prayers in a variety of places. When they were not able to worship in the Temple, they gathered in the synagogue on the Sabbath and on Feast Days to read the Word of God, to profess their faith, and to pray. The Israelites also prayed regularly at home—in the morning, at noon, and at night.

The most special place of prayer was the Temple of Jerusalem, where sacrifices were offered and where the great Feast Days were solemnly celebrated to commemorate the miraculous interventions of God throughout history, beginning with Passover.

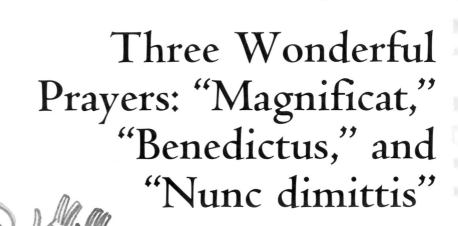

Three Wonderful Prayers: "Magnificat," "Benedictus," and "Nunc dimittis"

The righteous had waited, praying for the coming of Jesus, the Messiah and Savior, and when he came, prayer became more alive and intense. Scripture has given us three prayers born from the experience of being close to Jesus. After the Lord's Prayer, these are the most beautiful prayers in the entire Bible, and the Church repeats them every day with deep emotion.

The first of these prayers is the "Magnificat," which burst forth from the humble heart of Mary, the Mother of Jesus. God chose her so that he could do "great things" through her, and the Magnificat is her prayer of gratitude to him.

The second prayer is the "Benedictus." It was offered up by Zacharias, the father of John the Baptist, in praise of God's merciful goodness.

The third prayer, the "Nunc dimittis," sprang forth from the relieved soul of the elderly Simeon. The Holy Spirit had told Simeon that he would not die until he had seen the Messiah. When Simeon had taken the baby Jesus in his arms in the Temple, he asked the Lord to let him leave this world in peace.

The Prayer of Jesus

When Jesus came, everything was made new, even prayer. Jesus addressed his prayers to God, his Father, to whom he gave himself with love and devoted joy. Indeed, Jesus spent his life in prayer. He dedicated the quiet and lonely hours of the evening to loving conversation with his Father. And he turned to him during the important moments of his mission on earth and before he performed miracles, giving thanks to the Father and petitioning him with the confidence that his prayers would be heard.

The prayer of Jesus during his agony before his crucifixion is moving and dramatic. Although he begs his Father to save him from the cross, he obediently entrusts himself to his Father's will. He accepts death as an act of love to the Father as well as an act of intercession and supplication for the salvation of all humanity.

"Knock and the door will be opened to you"

Jesus was not the only one who prayed. He also urged his disciples to turn to the Father in his name, confident that God would listen to them as his children. They were to pray with humility, sincerity, patience, and trust. Jesus encouraged them to pray by telling them the parables of the insistent friend who continued to ask for something to eat in the dead of night until he was satisfied, and of the persevering widow who repeatedly asked for justice. Just as these requests were answered, Jesus said, God would answer the disciples' persistent prayers.

Jesus himself answered prayers that had been prayed in faith: he restored the sight of the blind, he made the crippled walk, and he made lepers clean again.

"Lord, teach us to pray": The Lord's Prayer

The disciples could have learned to pray by listening to Jesus while he prayed. But one day one of them specifically asked him, "Lord, teach us to pray."

Jesus satisfied this request by teaching his disciples the Lord's Prayer. This prayer, which we pray every day, is a summary of all the important elements of the Gospel. However, the Lord did not just leave us words with which to address the Father. Most importantly, he gave us the gift of his Spirit, which filled our hearts with the kind of love that children have for their father. Thus, we too can share in the prayer of Jesus himself, the Son of God.

Saint Paul tells us that "God sent the Spirit of his Son into our hearts, crying out, 'Abba, Father!'" (Gal. 4:6). It is the Spirit who stirs the desire for prayer in us, and then tells us what to ask in prayer. Even when we pray by ourselves, we never pray alone: we are always in the presence of Jesus and the Holy Spirit.

The Lord's Prayer is the main prayer of the Church, and the prayer prayed most often. It is the model for all other prayers. It is a prayer we should know by heart, so that we can meditate on it deeply and pray it often: it should inspire and shape our entire existence. A true Christian lives the Lord's Prayer.

It will be helpful to examine this prayer more closely and explain it line by line.

*Our Father,
who art
in heaven,
hallowed be
thy name;
thy kingdom
come;*

In communion with Jesus, we address God with the confidence of children who are greatly loved by their Father and who have become one family in him.

With both humility and joy, we invoke God with "Our Father." We also ask that the holiness of God be recognized by all people, and that the Lord Jesus, who is already present among us, will come again in glory and in this way definitively bring to fulfillment the reign of God.

*thy will
be done
on earth
as it is
in heaven.*

The will of
God is his
mysterious plan
of love in action
in the world. In the
third petition of the
Lord's Prayer, we ask that this plan be fulfilled and
that we accept it with faith, willingly submitting to
it in every circumstance of our lives: in daily work,
in health and in sickness, in the various and difficult trials that the Lord may allow in our lives.

In this petition we also ask for
insight into God's plan for us, as well
as strength to accept this plan. Jesus is
always the model of how to do what
God wills: in every moment, he is busy
doing what is pleasing to the Father.

Give us this day
our daily bread;
and forgive us
our trespasses,

Vignatia

as we forgive those who trespass against us;

Because we are God's children, and he is the Father who provides for us, we ask him with trust for the bread that we need each day to survive. We ask for it for ourselves and for those who are dear to us, with whom we are called to share it. This bread represents everything that we need.

We also need to have God forgive our sins, but in order to receive divine pardon, we must be willing to always forgive others.

and lead us not
into temptation,
but deliver us
from evil.
Amen.

Because of our weakness, it is easy for us to give in to temptation. Recognizing this, we beseech the Father to keep us from yielding to temptation, and to make us participants in the victory of Jesus over the Tempter. We must always be on guard, because the Evil One will always be seeking to ensnare us. He is not just an imaginary figure or a symbol of evil. Jesus called him "a murderer from the beginning," "a liar and the father of lies," and "the prince of this world." Jesus threw him out of heaven, but he can still tempt us to sin. We therefore ask Jesus to deliver us from him.

The Lord's Prayer ends with "Amen," which means "So be it." That single word summarizes all of the desire we have expressed to God and all of our trust in him.

The Church at Prayer

The followers of Jesus are faithful to the teaching and commands of their Teacher. They often gather to pray; indeed, the Church is a praying community. If the Church did not pray, it would lose its identity and would no longer be the Church of Christ.

The most solemn and important form of prayer is the liturgy. Here the faithful gather together with the priest to commemorate the works of the Lord, beginning with his passion, death, and resurrection, which are the principal mysteries of our salvation.

For this reason, the most important prayer of the Church is the celebration of the Eucharist, in which we commemorate the Easter mystery and the body and blood of Jesus are really present.

Other important occasions for prayer are the celebration of the other sacraments, and the Liturgy of the Hours, in which the various times of the day are made holy, particularly by praying specially chosen Psalms.

Jesus himself is always present in liturgical prayer, uniting his Church to the prayer that he unceasingly raises to the Father.

Sunday
Prayer
and
Daily
Prayer

The
Church gathers
together in prayer par-
ticularly on Sunday, the Lord's
Day. On this day we commemorate the
resurrection of Jesus, we receive his body and
blood, we raise our praise to the Father, and we
share the joy of renewing our mutual love. In addition to Sunday, there are other Feast Days of the
Liturgical Year that are solemn days of prayer.

There is another community in which the
followers of Christ pray: the family, which has
been called the "Domestic Church."

Finally, each of us says our daily prayers,
particularly at the beginning and the end of
the day, so that the day opens and closes in the
name of the Lord.

Communal Prayer
and Personal Prayer;
Spoken Prayer
and Silent Prayer

The Lord's followers also pray in contexts other than the liturgy and family prayers. There is prayer with a small group of others, for which Jesus specifically promises his presence. And there is personal prayer, which we offer up in our "inner room," with the door closed, under the gaze of the Father, "who sees in secret" (Matt. 6:5-6). But even private personal prayer is part of the prayer of the entire Church.

Prayer must always come from the heart. We can raise our voices in spoken prayer. But it is also possible to pray silently, by directing our minds to God and allowing our souls to adore him.

Prayers

In addition to the Lord's Prayer, there are other prayers that are cherished and prayed often in the Church — prayers that are brief, simple, and to the point.

Some prayers are directed to the Holy Trinity, others to the Virgin Mary. There is a prayer to our Guardian Angel, and a prayer for the dead. There are morning and evening prayers, and prayers to be said before meals.

It is a good idea to memorize these prayers, so that we can easily and frequently pray them, either by speaking them aloud or, even better, by meditating on them in our hearts.

The Sign of the Cross
In the name of the Father
and of the Son
and of the Holy Spirit.
Amen.

Glory Be to the Father

Glory be to the Father,
and to the Son,
and to the Holy Spirit.
As it was in the beginning,
is now, and ever shall be,
world without end.
Amen.

The Hail Mary

Hail Mary, full of grace,
the Lord is with thee.
Blessed art thou among women,
and blessed is the fruit
of thy womb, Jesus.
Holy Mary, Mother of God,
pray for us sinners, now,
and at the hour of our death.
Amen.

Angel of God

Angel of God,
my guardian dear,
to whom God's love
commits me here.
Ever this day be at my side,
to light and guard,
to rule and guide.
Amen.

Eternal Rest

Eternal rest
grant unto them, O Lord.
And let perpetual light
shine upon them.
May they rest in peace.
Amen.

Morning Prayer

I adore you, my God,
and I love you with all my heart.
I thank you for having created me,
for having made me a Christian,
and for having protected me
during the night. I offer you what
I do this day: may all my actions be
in accordance with your divine will, and for your greater
glory. Protect me from sin and from all evil. May your
grace always be with me and with those dear to me. Amen.

Blessing of Food

Bless us, O Lord,
and these your gifts,
which we are about to receive
from your bounty.
Through Christ our Lord.
Amen.

Evening Prayer

I adore you, my God,
and I love you with all my heart.
I thank you for having created me,
for having made me a Christian,
and for having protected me
during this day. Forgive me the sins
that I have committed today, and if I have done some good,
accept it. Protect me during my sleep, and free me from all
danger. May your grace always be with me and with those
dear to me. Amen.

Hail Holy Queen

Hail, holy Queen, Mother of
Mercy. Hail, our life, our sweetness,
and our hope. To thee do we cry,
poor banished children of Eve; to
thee do we send up our sighs,
mourning and weeping, in this
valley of tears. Turn then, most gracious advocate, thine
eyes of mercy toward us; and after this our exile, show
unto us the blessed fruit of thy womb, Jesus. O clement,
O loving, O sweet Virgin Mary.

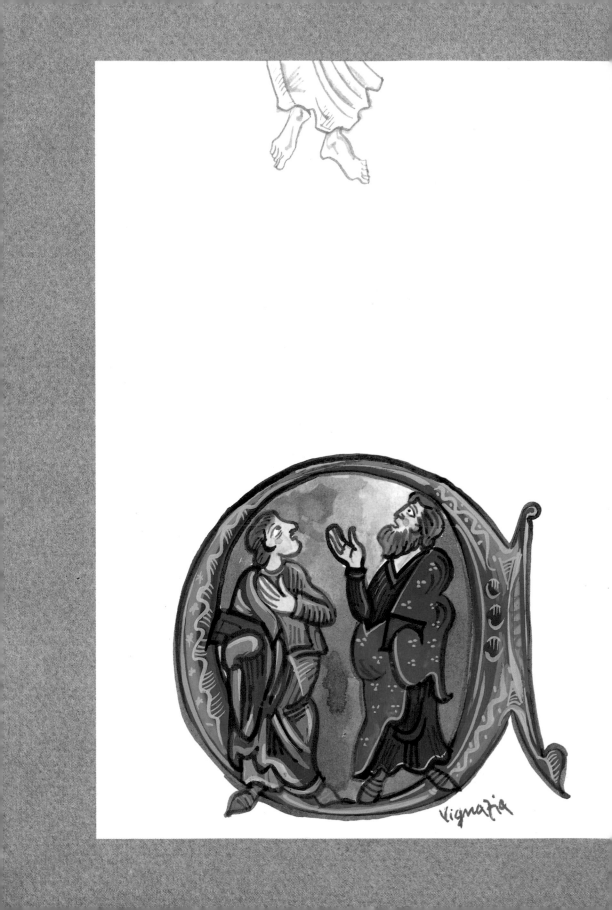